"Amy is well-practiced in perceiv_ _ _ _ _ _ _ _ _ _ _ _ _ glory of God in the midst of the ordinary and the extraordinary, in suffering and beauty, scarcity and abundance. In this exquisite collection of poems, she opens for us a portal and invites us to come and behold our own belovedness in the heart of God. Reading her work is an opportunity for worship. I will savor these poems again and again."

—**SHARON GARLOUGH BROWN,**
author of the *Sensible Shoes* series and *Shades of Light* series

"To hear the kind of music offered by nature's choristers, amid an infinite world of competing voices, a listener needs a focus of intention and attention. This is the task of every poet, and this is Amy Nemecek's calling and vocation. In this brilliant transcription of responsive poems we are reminded of the generous beauty offered us by our Creator, if we would only look and listen, if we would join in offering praise. Read these lovely verses and give thanks."

—**LUCI SHAW,**
author of *Angels Everywhere* and *The Generosity*

"I've had the great pleasure of taking a walk in the woods with Amy Nemecek. Her pace is of one not eager to win a race but of one hoping to see . . . hear . . . feel . . . know. She's someone who marvels at dewy understory and takes great delight in a sparrow's song. I've also had the great pleasure of reading Amy's poetry. Her work is tender, insightful, brilliant. Readers can't help but see, hear, and feel the world as the poet experiences it. Perhaps best of all is the way in which readers will encounter a sense of knowledge—both knowing the heart of the work and being known by it. What a gift that is."

—**SUSIE FINKBEINER,**
author of *The Nature of Small Birds* and *All Manner of Things*

"Poetry is a creative art form that moves us past mere cognition and below depth of feeling into a profound knowing and being known. Amy's poems shepherded my soul into a wondrous journey. I was inspired, transported, and seen. I highly recommend these poems to you. Enjoy how they will expand your own heart."

—**GEM FADLING,**
founding partner of Unhurried Living, Inc., and author of *Hold That Thought*

"Rub dust on your palms, pluck the ripened sunshine, and taste this poetic grace. I can't wait to receive Amy's printed collection into my hands."

—**DWIGHT BAKER,**
president and CEO of Baker Publishing Group

Amy Nemecek

# The Language of the Birds

## and other poems

IRON
PEN

PARACLETE PRESS
BREWSTER, MASSACHUSETTS

2022 First Printing

*The Language of the Birds: and Other Poems*

Copyright © 2022 by Amy Nemecek

ISBN 978-1-64060-787-3

The Iron Pen name and logo are trademarks of Paraclete Press.

Library of Congress Cataloging-in-Publication Data
Names: Nemecek, Amy, 1974- author.
Title: The language of the birds : and other poems / Amy Nemecek.
Description: Brewster, Massachusetts : Paraclete Press, 2022. | Summary:
  "The author reflects on the larger themes of beauty, loss, motherhood, family, and vocation as she contemplates the sacredness of ordinary moments." -- Provided by publisher.
Identifiers: LCCN 2022018996 (print) | LCCN 2022018997 (ebook) | ISBN
  9781640607873 (trade paperback) | ISBN 9781640607880 (epub) | ISBN
  9781640607897 (pdf)
Subjects: BISAC: POETRY / Subjects & Themes / Inspirational & Religious |
  POETRY / American / General | LCGFT: Poetry.
Classification: LCC PS3614.E45243 L36 2022  (print) | LCC PS3614.E45243
  (ebook) | DDC 811/.6--dc23/eng/20220525
LC record available at https://lccn.loc.gov/2022018996
LC ebook record available at https://lccn.loc.gov/2022018997

10 9 8 7 6 5 4 3 2 1

Published by Paraclete Press
Brewster, Massachusetts
www.paracletepress.com

Printed in the United States of America

*In loving memory of my parents,*
*Richard & Julia Houskamp*

*"The lines have fallen to me in pleasant places;*
*Indeed, my heritage is beautiful to me."*
PSALM 16:6

# CONTENTS

## 1

## 2

# 3

1

# The Language of the Birds

On the fifth day, your calloused fingers
stretched out and plucked a single reed
from the river that flowed out of Eden,
trimmed its hollow shaft to length and
whittled one end to a precise vee
that you dipped in the inkwell of ocean.
Touching pulpy nib to papyrus sky,
you brushed a single hieroglyph—
feathered the vertical downstroke
flourished with serif of pinions,
a perpendicular crossbar lifting
weightless bones from left to right.
Tucking the stylus behind your ear,
you blew across the wet silhouette,
dried a raven's wings against the static,
and spoke aloud the symbol's sounds:
"Fly!"

# Beloved

You have carved, chiseled, tattooed
me on the palms of your hands.
*Yud. Dalet.* Two Hebrew runes
christen me cherished, adored,
favored, precious. Beloved, let us
love one another. Dearly beloved,
we are gathered here together.
In the high and far-off times,
O Best Beloved. My beloved is
mine and I am his. Indelible,
undeniable identity.

I put mirrored palms together,
raise them out and up in praise,
reminding you, reminding myself,
that I am a marked woman, forever
branded by the etchings of your grace.

# Hidden Manna

Your manifesto is everywhere manifest, a
samizdat song the Spirit gives ears to hear
in nebulae pillars we view via Hubble,

newborn stars clutched by hydrogen talons;
in electron cloud octets, minuscule infinity
compressed between swiftly tilting shells;

in the scratching quill of a monk turned
outlaw, sequestered by Wartburg's walls;
in Pascal's scribbled blaze secretly sewn

to the lining of his coat (he died and his life
is hidden with Christ in God); in the Gospel
of John copied on backs of postage stamps

and smuggled into Soviet gulags; in the
half ichthus traced by a dirt-crusted toe,
its dusty reply mirroring silent solidarity.

And I will ask the Father, and he will give
you hidden manna, loaves and fish to store
in hearts and minds against the day of want.

# Petoskey Stones

If you go too fast, you'll miss
hexagonal supernovas staring
up at you from the beach. But
if you walk slowly, you'll bow
often to pluck ordinary rocks
from wet sand's gray obscurity,
rinse them clear in turquoise
shallows, lock eyes with
cherubim that lift your gaze
further down, deeper in to
where wheels within wheels
of fossilized coral swirl in the
palm of your hand, flinging
ancient sunbursts across the
waves to the four corners
of this mighty inland sea.

# Adam's Rib

First Adam's eyes grew heavy
closed in sleep like death
while omnipotent knife-hand
slid surgically into thoracic cavity
extracted a single rib, closed
incision without stich or scar
sculpted curves and contours
thighs hips breasts neck
brought her to the man
who said, "Bone of my bone
and flesh of my flesh; she shall
be called Woman because
she was taken out of Man."

Second Adam's eyes grow dim
close in sleep-like death
spear scalpels between two ribs
precision punctures myocardium
spilling blood lymph water air
omniscient fingers knit
gaping wound into glorified scar
craft flesh and bone into Church
give her to the Given One
who says, "Blood of my blood
and body of my body; she shall
be called Bride because
she is taken out of Bridegroom."

# Companion

*after Van Gogh's* Starry Night

Hovering over the face of the deep,
I join you in its convex solitude.
You shrug a melancholy shroud
around sequestered shoulders,
turn inward past forsaken streets
to a single tallow prayer you left
burning at the altar. It gutters out
as you gaze beyond window bars,
inhale paint's painful perfume, begin
filling emptiness with impasto incense.

If I had called the night day,
your dark would not be lighter.

Hovering over the face of your palette,
we blend the pigments in tandem,
brushing cobalt hills to break against
ultramarine expanse, its otherworldly
whorl of cirrus whitecaps blazing.
I cup spirit hands above smoky umber
cypress, blow on citron moon that
quickens to planets, quasars, nebulae
searing heaven's concave canvas.

If I had called the darkness light,
your night could not be brighter.

# Bethlehem / Aleppo

Eyes turn to you, battered city, as in
your dark streets shine mothers' tears

while children huddle in hope and fear
after years of war. How silently we look

away as tiny kings who out-Herod Herod
send soldiers to slaughter innocents

seeking shelter, a hundred souls
together in bombsight crosshairs.

Two millennia and three hundred
miles removed from another town

ravaged, Rachel's tears still mingle
with her children's blood, the ache

of her keening carried on wind
and tide and satellite television,

inconsolable at her helplessness
to save them from rubble ruins.

# Fixer Upper

Saint Andrew and I ask in unison,
"Rabbi, where are you staying?"
*Come and see*, the Teacher beckons,

so I follow him to a stucco-smeared
façade that looks condemned, empty,
but he insists it's the place he abides.

He unlocks a rasping deadbolt into this
ramshackle clay shell that reeks of piss.
Everywhere is crumbling plaster, greasy

avocado tile, loose floorboards, moldy
popcorn ceilings, cracked leaded glass.
Foxes have dens, birds of the air have nests,

and the Son of Man chooses to dwell here?
He patiently walks me around its rooms,
lifts the corners of crusted orange shag

to reveal original hardwoods underneath,
points an experienced finger at potential:
knock out that wall, open up the kitchen,

install custom cabinets, French doors,
and double-hung, triple-pane windows.
It's a full-on restoration, not a quick flip.

And as I begin to see through his expert eyes,
I trust the Carpenter of hope to make all things,
even this renovation of my heart, better than new.

# Transfiguration

We followed him
to the top of this
great, high Mountain,
grew heavy-eyed,
footsore. I stuck
one of those
barking dogs
into my open
mouth before
cloud-command
could shut it fast.

When our fathers
approached this
holy Mountain,
brushing a blade
of grass meant death.
Now the Mountain
clasps my shoulder,
tousles John's hair,
side-hugs James.
We follow him down,
very much alive.

# Ash Wednesday

Words become dust before the ink dries.
So bitter breezes won't diffuse frail letters,
I smudge syllables with my thumb,
collect spent cinders in loops & whorls,
press them to your forehead in a cross
pronouncing you a poem penned by God.
Scatter, then, these ashes of my heart
across pages scorched by Spirit flame.

# Palm Sunday 2017

*"Egypt's Coptic churches hit by deadly blasts on Palm Sunday"*
*(BBC News, 9 April 2017)*

Green branches cut in their prime
land layered on consecrated table.
This your Body, broken even for those
of us sitting on upholstered pews,
our cushioned communion free from fear.

And this your shed blood tracing
seams between ancient flagstones,
scarlet smearing cream columns
that flank choir and priests preparing
to serve bread and wine and Word.

From the blood of innocent Abel
calling out from saturated sod,
to the blood of Zechariah, whom
ISIS detonated between sanctuary
and altar, we remember your death.

And we know your grave is empty,
but ours remain so full.

# Servant

A great man once said he wasn't worthy
to untie my sandals, so I remove them myself,
rise from the table, seamlessly slip off my coat,

hang it on a peg behind the door, then fill
a wooden bowl, snag a towel from the floor.
Twenty-four eyes shift right, left, right.

At any other meal I'd crack a joke,
but not tonight. Twelve jaws set tight.
I kneel before Andrew, place his two feet

in my lap, work loose stubborn laces.
Resistant tarsals recoil as I lave cool
water over calloused soles. I dry one

then the other, move down a line
of chapped heels, flat arches, bunions,
broken nails, blisters, gritty toe jam.

My Peter protests, tucks his legs away,
insists I bathe his head and hands,
but finally yields to apostolic ablutions.

When I move to Judas, he stands,
side-steps my example, sloshes the
sludgy basin in his haste to leave.

Dropping the filthy rag on his
deserted cushion, I reclaim my robe
and resume my place as Host.

# Wheat

*"Satan has asked to sift you as wheat. But I have prayed for you . . . that your faith may not fail." (LUKE 22:31–32)*

Permission granted,
sifting begins as
our Master withdraws alone,
leaving me to guard the threshing floor.
Sleep proves too strong a foe
for eyelids that droop amid
snores of fellow laborers.
"Simon. Simon!"

The enemy is already at the door,
violent waking from idylls
of power, riches, praise.
My flailing sword fells an ear.
I swing for another, but one
command mutes brashness
I spoke at a sprint:
"I will never fall away!"

Bonfires outline familiar features.
Fears of recognition realized,
I'm damned to discovery.
Venomous curses and vicious oaths
invoke the name of the One I deny.
Rooster's crow keens loud and long
while dawn delays.
"I do not know the man!"

Kernel exposed, red wind drives away
chaff, leaving only the harvest
to be ground with a stone,
baked by the Bread of Life,
served on a beach with broiled fish.
Dead seed germinates under
questions of love.
"Feed my sheep."

# Rooster Crow

Tradition tells us, Peter, that
after one night's disavowal
you never heard morning's
call without mourning.

At rooster crow you went out
and wept bitterly, and its sound
forever triggered startled sobs,
like waking from dreams of falling.

Yet I wonder, the prisms that
glisten on your eyelids now,
faraway failures refracted in rheumy lens,
whether these are laments of gratitude,

of bitter joy that despite denial
his mercies are new every morning.
Embrace, then, this alarum,
this waking to his great faithfulness.

# Pentecost

On this fiftieth day since Easter
we expected fire. We got snow.
We expected winter's grip to loose
long before our mid-May celebrations,
but graupel bounces like live coals
on the deck and begins to blanket
the yard I've mowed twice already.

I don't want to preach like Peter or
speak in tongues of men and angels.
Only let me listen as ice-hot wind batters
my heart inside out, let Spirit-blown
flakes kiss my forehead, sear my tongue,
cauterize my words with frigid heat.
Mute the Babel of voices into white
noise until all I sense is the breath
of the Comforter's coming.

# Lines on Holbein's Portrait of Calvin

*"To you, O Lord, I offer my heart, promptly and sincerely."*
—John Calvin

From the time I was eight I have pondered
your portrait, felt your finger pointing at me,
punctuating each petaled syllable
of your theological bouquet
so I could recite them in my sleep.

Your rigid words, stoic pose,
painted stare intimidated me,
like the look my mother gave
(and I now give my son)
for fidgeting in church.

For years I searched and turned away
from what Geneva's Genius had to say,
until I saw the slimmest smile—
not scolding but proud, the teacher
attending his pupil's commencement.

Your gesture no longer accuses or alarms
but points to One who works all things.
I follow your gaze to my parents' faith,
mine now, and keep my hand-held heart
ready, reaching in offering to Christ.

# Grand Canyon

Undeterred by danger signs
or Day-Glo safety barriers
she toed the South Rim's lip,
plunged her eyes a mile down,
nudged a red rock over the edge
to hear its clattering fall.

When it comes to the canyon
of her own heart, however,
she's less brash, unwilling
to step to the ridge, lean over,
and survey the depths of its
restless, rock-strewn wall.

# Recipes from a Food Pantry

Start with one small can of tuna—
only one because there are three people
in your household, not four.
Serve it on slices of toast from a frozen
bread loaf, its sell-by date long past.
Garnish with canned green peas (drained),
a squirt of ketchup, mustard, and relish
since the makeshift plywood
shelves held no mayo today.

If that doesn't satisfy, pour yourself
a bowl of toasty wheat, moisten
with a single-serving carton
of room-temperature rice milk,
interrupt its dry crisscross with raisins,
one item they had in abundance.

Dessert is a treat: vanilla pudding mix.
You're out of milk. You don't even have
powdered left from your last visit.
Substitute grapefruit juice, ruby red,
then stir in a dollop of generic jellied
cranberry sauce as if it's Thanksgiving.

For breakfast open the crunchy peanut butter
(you got the last jar) and spread it
with a smear of margarine
on a half stale English muffin.

Place your one jumbo roll of single-ply
on the dispenser by the toilet, ration it
square by square, and pray it lasts
until a week from Tuesday when
the Old Time Methodist church opens
its peeling white-painted doors again.

# ¡Gracias, Lucinda!

*(for the children of Lirio de los Valles, Aldama, Mexico)*

Joy in pigtails and faded purple shorts
takes my hand and pulls me to the
hard-packed haze that passes for a pitch.
Lucinda's too small and I'm too old
to play futbol with los gringos,
so we stand along the sidelines,
tossing a spongy ball between us.
Lucinda has little to call her own;
no shirt, no shoes, no parents,
nothing but a nombre, three saffron syllables
that summon sunshine in her smile.
Lucinda spots a bit of rojo on the ground,
plucks it with thumb and forefinger,
scours the dirt for more discarded beads.
Animated by chiaroscuro chatter,
her caramel eyes insist I help string
dusty handfuls of color on twine
scavenged from scraggly mesquite.
Lucinda schools me in the Spanish spectrum,
corrects my flat pronunciation.
Flourishing a finished bracelet,
she ties a half hitch around my wrist,
encircles me with friendship
in this home where patience nurtures,
mercy heals, justice and peace embrace.

# Revelation 2:17

What if the new name
you give me on that day
is just an old name I've
carried in my pocket,
a talisman fingered smooth
like the Tchaikovsky waltz
on repeat in my mind's ear,
its lilting five-four keeping
tempo with the waves?

What if the white stone
you hand me is familiar,
so that simply hearing
you whisper *Beloved*
makes it ever new?

# 2

# April Snow

Just yesterday children romped behind
privacy fences, and city streets reeked
of lighter fluid and charcoal briquets
and the first barbecues of an early spring.
Today I smell only fabric softener from
household dryer vents and menthol vapor
from the e-cigarette of a chilly neighbor
I pass six feet apart on the sidewalk.

My every exhalation creates a blizzard
of breath as wet flakes crust my shoulders
and collect in cups of panhandling tulips.
Red husks sloughed from maple buds
litter the pavement in a pulpy slush
of sodden slickness beneath my boots.

I pause in the parking lot of the shuttered
library where puddles mirror sky and trees
of a pre-pandemic universe. I dip my toes
in these glassy pools and yearn for a wood
between worlds that would transport me
to Narnia, Perelandra, Paradise Regained,
but my feet only ripple the image and
leave me standing in this quarantined
gray town on a silent planet
as empty and isolated as Charn.

# Arrowhead

I walk the banks of Buck Creek,
ears tuned to spring's torrent.

My son toddles ahead, arcs pebbles
over the rail, plunks concentric circles.

I palm a rock from damp decay,
rub it clean on my grass-stained jeans,

wind up to skip it across ripples
when my fingers detect intent—

chipped geometry chiseled to a shaky point,
notches carved to grip a shaft now dust.

I run a thumb along one edge, still sharp,
then slide the flinty poem in my pocket.

# It Is Well

Peace like a river eludes me—

My pilgrim heart pants hard
after water brooks, pauses

to refresh body and soul
by some rain-swollen stream.

Drizzled droplets accumulate
on cattails and cottonwoods,

elongate to tears that land
in slick ripples and plump

to rings, slip over rocks,
diffuse into freshet springs.

—so I'll be content with this creek.

# Counterpoint

A robin called at midnight.
Its articulated song streaked

orange cantabile east to west
over moon-shaped shadows.

Startled by its own voice,
it did not call again.

# Brittlebush
## (Encilia farinosa)

Praises poised in desert petals
deftly dance on slender stem;
eyes are lifted to the mountains
blessing him who hallows them

with soil and dew, sun and rain,
licorice fragrance wafting high,
silvered incense, sacred breaking
offer thanks for sand and sky.

# Memory Garden

*for Esther*

She's tended a garden since childhood,
her father's green thumb transplanted
on her DNA like heirloom perennials
cramming meticulous borders and beds.

Loam nourished through fruitful joy,
fallow grief, rests gnarled and numb
like the fingers that once tilled it.

Weed-free plots edged to persnickety
perfection succumb to sorrel,
purslane, thistle, and spurge
clamoring to overcreep bounds.

Two years ago she finally let her
neighbor mow the greening grass;
last year she forgot shrubs with clever
names like forsythia, spirea, weigela,
but still retained lilting sounds like
columbine, peony, and lupine.

This year primrose, poppy, puschkinia,
pinks, plants tended like children are
forgotten with scripture and songs.

Mercifully she recalls a few favorites:
lavender, lilac, lily of the valley.
Psalm 23. The Lord's Prayer.
The chorus of "O How I Love Jesus."

I pick a spring posy of crocus and daffodils
to brighten these four ecru walls.
Grass withers, flowers fade, but she smiles
at their purple and gold impermanence
even as she inhales a faraway
familiar scent that is Home.

# Weeds

I rip them out, roots and all, every chance I get,
seldom thinking of their names, and yet,
there's music in a sobriquet
like trefoil, chicory, heal all, mullein.

Adam delighted in naming animals, insects, flowers,
Eve, but when it came to naming weeds, each syllable
stung like nettles, knowing sorrel, purslane,
thistle seeds would infiltrate Eden's bowers.

# Summer Solstice

Pallid aspen
trunks strafe
stratus skies.
Midnight strobes
beg back light
beyond horizon
where sun set
minutes ago.

Percussions bound
between clouds
and ten thousand
lakes and valleys
of bleating sheep.

All's quiet.
Coyotes call.
A hundred dozen
fireflies blink
between raindrops,
echoing (echoing)
dawn's petrichor.

# How Much Blue?

Velvet jazz drifts across the lake from where an
ensemble plays at the pavilion, trumpet crooning,
*How much blue can summer hold?*

Dad's Ferguson tractor sits idle in the field, its
cadet-blue paint powdery from hours in the sun.
Dresses, towels, dungarees flap against cerulean sky,
blue on blue on blue to match the heron that fishes

in the neighbor's pond. Chicory grows in periwinkle
canyons along this country road. Skippers, sulphurs,
and brush-foots flit among bachelor's button.
Jays scold from turquoise-dusted spruce boughs.

We drive to the blueberry patch and fill buckets.
I love rolling their tartness around on my tongue
as I sit on the deck, a book of Mary Oliver's poems
open on my lap, its pages stained with dusk.

An azure dragonfly alights on the railing,
so close I could stroke its slender thorax.
Barn swallows and martins wing to roosts.
Procyon winks in twilight indigo.

More than enough.

# Graveside

In Laurel Grove one hot July,
I stood by the grave
of my great-great-grandfather,
watched you weave among gray granite
until you found two names held dear,
years of birth—years of death,
lifetimes contained in dashes.
Knowing you'd not pass this way again,
you knelt to brush grass from chiseled
sans serif cold under sweltering sun.

In Chapel Hill the next July,
we gathered at another garden
with a peaceful name that doesn't soothe,
said goodbye, planted you where
I now stand over a bronze slab,
years of birth—years of death,
my lifetime contained in dashes.
Wishing I'd never have to pass this way again,
I kneel to brush leaves from raised roman
capitals that spell out two names of my own.

# Late Summer Lyric

All manner of creeping things and flying things
and creeping-flying things seek a place to rest,
ease aching legs, weary wings.

Many-legged larvae, plump, limber,
stroll milkweed, spin havens of bejeweled green.
Striving takes a siesta as wings are woven,

perfectly mirrored sails that free them to find
more permanent dwellings beyond November.

# Hummingbird

You're leaving again, aren't you?
I can tell by the way you spend entire
minutes perched on my shepherd's
hook, the red feeder's plastic flower
beacons inviting you to binge.
We make eye contact as you peer
in the window by my desk. Do you
wonder what these scribbles mean?

All summer you've sipped sugar water
I replenish each sun-dappled week.
Today you guzzle, filling reserves
that will carry your tiny body south,
south, ever south. One more preen
of your delicate feathers, their
green faded with August foliage,
then you hover low and are gone.
I'll miss you. At least you said good-bye.

# Climbing Glastonbury Tor

I'm falling up to Avalon's shore,
drawn by emerald clarion.
Green calls to green at Spirit-wind's roar
gusting from heights of Albion.

Ascending shade to shade, I seize
this verdant blaze of mystery.
Mythlore scents the ancient breeze,
mingles with England's history.

# Streets of Gold

*In heaven it is always autumn,*
*His mercies are ever in their maturity.*
—JOHN DONNE

Who says the golden paths we'll walk
are paved with cold, hard ingots?
My feet fly over a roadbed of coins

that flutter from aspens in perfectly
heart-shaped currency. For all the leaves
descending, the wealth does not deplete,

branches are never cold and bare,
but always warm and glowing,
like flames on an autumn hearth.

# Acedia

When aspen leaves turn gold,
you ride in on a whirlwind
to a diner called Nowhere,
snap down your kickstand,
sling helmet over handlebars.
You side-hug me and grin as
we enter this smalltown café
and claim a glitter-red booth,
its vinyl tacky with duct tape.
I feed the juke box quarters
and select the Beach Boys,
then slide across from you.
We split an order of onion rings,
reminisce between bites of burgers,
cry over a spilled milkshake. I feel
so broke up, I want to go home.

I'm about to say how God only
knows what I'd be without you,
when the needle sticks on
Sloop John B.'s bridge, and
you pick up the check and aim
for the door. My pilgrim heart
remains, stirring questions
and single-serve creamers
into my coffee as I watch you
straddle your V-twin cherubim,
ignite them with a roar, then
twist the throttle until the road
rises up between you and me
and my longing for more.

# October

comes in
couplets
stanzas
entire sonnets
each floating leaf
a syllable
word
phrase
in nature's lyric
oak
maple
beech
aspen
flutter-fall
land in metered layers
on forest floor
collect in quatrains
of crimson, gamboge, gold
acorn and pinecone
sestinas lisp
autumn susurrus
as crisp lines crunch
iambic feet
beneath my boots.

# Hope Deferred

I arrive late without a lesson plan,
two things a teacher must never do,
yet I find myself perpetually
unprepared this divisive November.
*How long, O Lord?*

My Sunday school students teeter
on metal chairs around a folding
table as perforated boredom
shutters their eyelids.
*Will you look away forever?*

My sentry heart grows footsore
watching for the dawn.

# Larch Song

Just when I think it's over,
when October rains silence
autumn's symphony and
mute the forest brown,
tamarack voices crescendo
in coniferous plainchant
of yellow needles, their
dorian modality rising
to golden fortissimo
along November roads
before snow cues a
deciduous diminuendo
that drones sepia sotto voce.

# Grapefruit

I slice the golden corona in two,
revealing backlit rose windows
mirrored across the plate's transept
and sending up juicy flares of pulp.
These ruby rays may be the only
sunshine I see today, so I will indulge.
Yes, I will slit membranes
to separate gleaming wedges,
scoop sepals to my tingling tongue,
squeeze liquid light from empty rind,
my salivary glands contracting as I
savor drops of summer in December.

# Winter Solstice

I wake while it's dark
and lie in bed waiting,
eager to welcome wan rays.
Dawn delays.

I rise, brew coffee, press
my husband's shirt and pants
as a boys' choir warbles on the radio.
Light lags.

Without warning, sunrise.
Snow turns gray
      blue
    white.
It's hard to keep watch
when two-thirds of day
is night.

# Melancholidays

The face of this year reads five minutes till next,
and again I confront the holidays an orphan.
For the twentieth time I think I can't, until shining eyes
plead for me to pull red totes from beneath the stairs,
deck the halls with tinsel wreaths, unpack the
creche from its tissue paper wrappings.
We string the tree with blue LEDs that
twinkle joy as you choose ornaments to dangle
on fragrant fir fingers dripping with dazzle.
We drink cocoa and eggnog while watching
Rudolph and Frosty and *The Sound of Music.*
I pull Mom's recipes from the battered tin box,
cream memories with butter and sugar and flour,
then slip a Bing Crosby CD in the player because I miss
her and Dad, and somehow that indigo voice crooning
"I'll be home for Christmas" soothes the ache of their absence.

I do all this for you, my son, because they did this for me.
Grandpa & Grandma gleam in your yuletide cheer.
Their faces reflect in the window of your smile.

# Sunset—Epiphany

twilight.

hills into

draw eastern

drops in topmost twigs

suspend liquid light

up tree trunks

ooze honeyed rays

circle bottle-glass horizon

elongated shadows

angled west

sweetness through a straw

Savor sun-soaked

# Like Eating a Plum

*"Michiganders have barely seen the sun since December"*
(GRAND RAPIDS PRESS, *January 30, 2017*)

When sunshine is measured
in minutes, not hours or days
you have to pluck it as soon as it's ripe
open the door to an icebox yard
snatch light from a blue-sky bowl
sink teeth into the pulpy golden orb
turning white snow dazzling
slurp suck savor every delicious ray
so sweet and so cold
spit the pale bare stone
behind another round of gray.

# February Lament

I crave green.
My bones ache for it in a dry and wintry land.
Soul scurvy propels me to floral aisles
when I do the weekly shopping.
I stroll between potted palms,
immerse my face in cut roses,
bask among Boston ferns,
finger waxy ficuses.
Hothouse flora doesn't hold fragrance, though
eyes tropically trick nose with suggestions of spring.
Once I've found each item on my list,
I'll linger in the produce department,
fawn over lettuce, leeks, kale, collards,
drop a rainbow of chard into my basket.
What warm winter fields did it grow in,
and how was I sown here?

# Standing Stones

I hear them before I see them:
sandhill cranes, their blowsy
laughter shrieking sharpened
joy among the keening canes.
Nine of them form a dolmen,
slender sarsens tabled under
the slate of morning mist
as they glean fallow furrows
of corduroy loam prickled
with last harvest's leavings.
When I attempt to approach
their sacred circle, they
vanish into silence.

# Gulfside Homily

Listen to the waves:
grace, grace, grace,
sometimes sighing,
sometimes crashing
hope in continual coming,
retreating, uniting
crest and trough,
mercy's amplitude.

Grace in sunlit whitecaps.
Grace in dolphins of moonlight
breaching midnight swells.
All your breakers and billows go over me,
pounding, drowning me until
I can't breathe for your goodness
surging, sucking, pulling me under
with rip currents of delight.

Grace as far as east from west,
as far as north from south.
Grace in sky above,
in ocean before.
Grace on beach beneath,
shell shards underfoot.
Grace to distant shore.

Listen to the grace,
lapping, slapping, licking bare toes;
laughing, squeaking sand psalms
along this ribbon of blue where
surf meets wet-packed tarmac of eternity.

# The lake is liquid again

Only last week bundled figures
crouched around holes in solid surface
or sped across on snow machines.

Overnight, slick silver dulled to flat steel
mumbling of danger before uncovering
deceptive blue bereft of waves.

Now, on the tenth of March, molecules
are set in motion as water's constant coming
beckons summer, when hulls will dot and dash

a leisurely telegraphy, and feet will splash
where sand and wet collide,
frolicking in their fluid game of tag.

# Stigmata

Spun-glass treetops scatter dawn's glow.
Red-breasted robins cluster below,
Crimson wounds on Easter snow.

# 3

# Ecclesiology 101

Nine of us take up a whole row.
I'm wedged between my parents.
The bare backs of my thighs
peel from the creaking pew
when we all stand to sing.
My mother lifts me until
my white-sandaled feet
are tiptoeing the bench
and my eyes are level
with Dad's sandpaper chin.
Her right hand steadies me,
his left hand holds a hymnal.
I slide to sitting for the sermon,
measure minutes watching
a wall-mounted fan oscillate
Dad's neat-slicked part
into a schoolboy cowlick.
God's here, and he smells
like spray starch, shaving soap,
Old Spice, and the wintergreen
candy that powders Dad's
pocket in sticky sweet pink.

# My Grandmother's Breakfast

She pulls a juicy sun from a mesh bag on the counter,
rolls it between her palms, carves it into equal hemispheres.
Plating one, its ruby carpels glowing like a rose window
in January's glim dawn, she carries it to the table
where a bowl of cereal awaits her daily rites.

She settles heavily into a spindle-back chair,
adjusts skirt and stockings, picks up a paring knife
and slides its slender blade around circumference
to separate fruit from rind, then cuts either side of
tracery membranes, releasing supple panes.

After she's savored each acidic wedge, the empty
peel is a limp asterisk she folds halfwise, squeezes
pulpy dregs spoon by careful spoonful. Only then
will she enjoy soggy squares bobbing in milk,
sweet to follow sour, never the other way round,
and sip scalding amens of coffee, benedictions on the day.

# Dad never reads poetry, except

the Psalms and Hallmark cards he buys
Mom for her birthday. He spends his time
tinkering with two-stroke Maytag motors,
rebuilding the engine on his Model T Ford,
resuscitating elegiac tractors.

Dad composes sonnets with grease
and gears, the rhyme scheme and
rhythm of carburetors and camshafts.
Mary Oliver mystifies him,
but he can scan the beat of his

Oliver baler while it chugs iambic
pentameter through summer hayfields,
baling twine knotting the end of every
line as green-gold verses slide off the chute
to land in perfectly spaced stubbled rows.

# Back to School

*"Children tie the feet." —Indian proverb*

That autumn morning my parents were footloose
once all six offspring boarded the bus.

I imagine them sitting side by side
on the bench seat of their brand-new car,

Dad's right arm draped around Mom's shoulders,
holding her close, his left hand relaxed over

the wheel as the V-8 engine powered
nineteen feet of American steel north.

I imagine Dad whistling as he steered
into the state park's vacant lot.

The only people for miles, they stopped
and rolled down the windows to enjoy

Lake Michigan breezes and a picnic lunch.
They'd never gone parking, but the empty

expanse of station wagon stretched
behind as the afternoon stretched before.

Lulled by the rhythm of pewter waves
slapping wet-packed sand, aroused by

warmth of September leaves and that
new-car smell, their fortysomething

selves united like twentysomethings.
I cruised along nine months later,

bonus baby conceived in the
back of a cranberry Oldsmobile,

a seventh loop in the silver cord
to twine their ankles fast.

# Vigil

We keep watch all through this night
of rented hospital bed and morphine drips,
brush damp hair off dew-cold brow,
touch moist sponge to parched lips,

Smooth hospital sheets, measure morphine drips,
hum "Blessed assurance, Jesus is mine,"
moisten sponge, touch parched lips
that thirst for flavors of glory divine.

You mouth "Jesus is mine, O what a foretaste,"
stare through darkened windowpanes,
hoping to glimpse moonlit glory, grace divine
in summer fields dotted with gray-green bales.

But pain narrows sight, vision wanes,
reminding us that all flesh is grass
rippling green-gray in summer fields;
our imperfect submission affords no rest.

Grassy days springing up with the sun
wither when malignant evening comes;
assured that Jesus is yours, you rest
while all through this night we keep watch.

# A Daughter's Keepsake

She used to brush my hair each night,
raking tangles free with her fingers
then stroking it smooth by lamplight.
Now I drape a fleece afghan over her legs,
move behind the chair to gently fluff
flat curls thinning faster than neurons.
Glints of silver reminisce in matted gray.
The steady caress of softness against scalp
quiets hands peeling imaginary potatoes.
I clean the bristles, fisting frizzled
threads of stories long unraveled.
Twisting some strands together, I tie them
with orange yarn, pocket the memento,
then press a kiss against parallel
grooves etched in her brow.
Back home, I find the paper packet
buried in her dresser drawer,
pull out one fat, golden curl
as thick as my thumb and tied
with a scrap of pink ribbon.
Laying the tokens side-by-side
on the vanity top, I pick up my
brush and begin skimming it
through my hair, but it's
her face I see in the mirror.

# For Jude

*"Her children rise up and bless her." (PROVERBS 31:28)*

You have a tender heart for strays,
whether kittens or starlings or students.

You shelter growing souls within walls
of words, paper, sturdy cover boards,

then clothe us with poetry and prose,
feed us letters and literature:
> Browning bread,
> a tall glass of *Middlemarch*,
> scoops of decadent Donne.

Some of us you choose to keep and call
your own. More than mentor, teacher,

you become mother, friend,
our stories indelibly inked

by the Author who printed all our
moments before time was typeset.

# Mechanics

Dad never wanted his daughter's hands to get dirty.
Still, he welcomed my presence each day after school,
and during the long days of summer vacation
he kept me busy stacking oil cans,
sorting parts, returning tools to the board,
sweeping floors, counting coins in his desk.
Along the way I watched and learned,
though not what you might think.

Now I fix books the way Dad fixed cars.
My wrench is a red pencil that I use
to install brakes in run-on sentences,
enrich the too-lean mixture of fragments,
insert commas so each sentence shifts smoothly.
I open the cover to look under the hood,
check the dipstick line-by-line,
kick the margins for proper inflation.
Sometimes it just needs a tune-up—
transpose crossed letters so they fire in order,
dot the i's and cross the t's for plenty of spark,
tweak the compound-complex timing of sentences.
Other times the engine is seized,
and a complete overhaul is in order.
That's when I pull whole paragraphs or chapters,
tear down and rebuild the transmission of ideas.

Dad didn't understand that ink
is just a different kind of grease
and his girl's fingers are filthy.

# September 11, 2001

We had just laid you on the altar
of inches and ounces and pounds
when the North Tower was hit.

The second plane struck the South
as a nurse poked your chubby thighs
with childhood immunizations.

We couldn't hear tragedy above your
cries, but I suckled you to soothe the hurt
and learned there's no vaccine for fear.

We were obliviously buckling you
into your rear-facing car seat
as the Pentagon burned.

By time we reached home
and turned on a TV, the whole
world had come crashing down.

We cradled you in our arms and wept.

# Chapter Break

The chatter flow subsides
and I find myself alone,
the *shish* of turning pages
all I hear in throbbing stillness
as my board book brain
ponders twelve-point type:

It can't talk back,
wipe off my kisses,
whine for the latest toy.

It isn't forever in motion;
serifs don't fidget or fuss
or jump on furniture.

Its rhetoric isn't punctuated
with karate kicks, wrestling throws,
or the gatling of pretend gunfire.

When I've had enough, I simply shut the cover
to stop the flow of sounds inside my head,
which reminds me that written words cannot
rub noses like Eskimoses, sink my battleship,
or gruggle a snoggy "I love you."

Still, their black-on-white crispness calms me
as I dogear another page in the story of Mom.

# Aslan Makes a Door in the Air

It wasn't there five minutes
ago when I still believed
you lived, prayed the
bleeding would stop, ached
to meet you in seven
months.

The ultrasound probe
penetrates my visions of
pigtails, pink swaddling,
Cabbage Patch dolls.
A heartbeat!

The nurse says it's mine.
Hope's final feather sinks
skeletal to forest floor
where a gentle-fierce Lion
sings a door.

Silent hinges swing
inward—you take
first steps away
instead of toward.
Tiny toes turn solid
over

silver threshold, bare
feet toddle to backlit
figures waiting past the
lintel to welcome you
further up, further in.

# Light Fantastic

*"What shall my West hurt me?"*
—JOHN DONNE, *"Hymne to God My God, In My Sicknesse"*

No matter how long I lie here,
you never take your green eyes off me.
I'm in your crosshairs and mustn't move

except to breathe. My chest is a map
where cosmographers now cluster,
charting their course in permanent ink.

Dimmed lights show $x$ and $y$ converge.
Latitude and longitude. North and south.
East and what? Shall my West hurt me?

Lines, numbers, angles mark the spot
where metal fingers focus photons,
fractions of light that caress and kill.

As you slow dance around me,
I close my eyes and surrender
to the clicking hum of your heels.

# Survivor Guilt

How do you think Job's servants felt
limping back to tally destruction?
*And I only am escaped alone to tell you...*
Each voice tapered, completing the litany of loss.
Their master tore his clothes,
caked his shorn, bleeding head with ashes,
grieved worship until his voice dried up.
They turned away, bewildered.

I slip out the door of the cancer wing
feeling healthy, strong, whole.
Today I'm the only one without an IV
snaking liquid hope into my veins.
*Am I only escaped alone to tell you?*
For six more months I'll hear the tolling
bell of family, friends, total strangers.
Listen as I write their names aloud.

# Only Child

*"Children are a gift from the L*ORD*; they are his reward. . . .*
*Blessed is the man whose quiver is full of them." (P*SALM *127:3)*

Sometimes we fling
that phrase as if singular
somehow means less,
as if only plural is gift.
I'm afraid it implies
you are not enough,
that solitary carries no blessing,
though we love to quote how
"God so loved the world
he gave his *only* son."

So cherish the label,
and always remember
you are more to us than
a dozen sons and daughters.
All our eggs are in one basket,
and we've given the basket to God.
You are his mighty arrow
who fills our quiver to bursting.
Into you we bend our strength
and pray you fly true.

# 3/2 Time

When I played piano as a child,
my hands struggled to cooperate,
and never more than when
the left played triplets,
the right played eighths,
my teacher counting
*one-lolly-two-lolly*
*one-and-two-and*
patient cues to play three over two.

Now that I'm a mother,
I struggle to coordinate
the duple of *Us*
with the triple of *We*,
knowing someday soon, Son,
you'll go solo, and once more these
fingers will fumble two notes per beat.
Then we'll long for the counterpoint
fugue you bring to every bar and phrase.

# Home Movies

I slide the homemade DVD into the player.
My sister labeled it "Holidays 1992" in black Sharpie.
Mom's face appears when I push play.

The camera follows her every move,
and I think how that must have hurt,
being the center of attention, because we all knew
but no one spoke aloud that this Christmas would be her last.

The voice I catch between grandkids' laughter is barely hers,
and I want you to know her, son, but not like this,
not the haunted look of cancer that even
her favorite red Christmas dress couldn't hide,
that our laughter and presents and denial couldn't defeat.
I want you to know her as she was.
So I write.

I write how your cousins climbed on her lap,
smothered her with kisses; how she blew raspberries
on adoring crimson cheeks and squeezed them tightly,
not wanting to let go, yet ready,
so ready, to fly.

# Prospect Park, Winter 1930

Out on the porch steps my mother would feed them
butter sandwiches, hot coffee, and yesterday's milk,
proffer last week's papers as insulation,

then point them on their transient way with a prayer.
They'd pound the pavement or ride the rails,
some young, some old, some sober, some not,

all sons, husbands, fathers, friends.
I suspect a secret hobo telepathy
signaled to stop at our door.

One beggar was about the age my brother would have been.
Mama gave him the coat out of Papa's closet—
the new topcoat he wore only to church,

heavy, soft, black, with gleaming buttons—
as if yards of costly cashmere would keep her firstborn warm.
My father was silent at supper.

"He looked so cold, Hen," I heard Mama say.
"You already have a coat for everyday.
Wear that to worship until we save for another."

On Sunday we walked through biting wind.
Papa turned up the frayed collar of his work jacket,
brushed at a grease-stained sleeve,

then slid his fist into the patched left pocket.
Passing the alley where men huddled around oil drums,
we glimpsed dark wool within the cluster.

Chapped fingers protruded from too-long sleeves,
stretched toward embers to hoard heat.
Papa squeezed my hand. Mama hugged his arm.

# Senior Prom 1945

There was a war on,
so she never thought
she'd go to the prom.
But when she walked in
from school that Friday
in May, her mother's love
hung clean and pressed,
a gown of white lawn that
twirled from the chandelier
over the dining room table.
Illusion layers shaped
a tea-length skirt.
Satin blushes trimmed
a sweetheart neckline.
Cap sleeves fluttered
in spring breezes from
open kitchen sashes.
A handsome sailor slipped
a circlet of pink carnations
around her trembling wrist
and escorted her to the dance.
If not for his dress blues
and spit-shined boots,
she'd have never thought
there was a war on.

# One Man's Trash

I see him every Friday when I drive
the only paved road to the village.
In ripped Levi's and Mossy Oak T-shirt
he browses among dust-brushed weeds
along the gravel shoulder, his sweat-stained
orange ball cap a beacon to passing cars.

He drags a black trash bag into which he
drops brown glass beer bottles, dented
aluminum cans he massages back to round,
green plastic two-liters, discarded water bottles.
He plods west, returns east, pausing every
hundred feet to retrieve another derelict dime
or nickel cast carelessly from open windows.

Once two bags bulge, he hauls his take
to the corner store, exchanges empties for cash,
enough to buy two scratch-and-wins, then
scores a pack of Marlboros, three Slim-Jims,
and a case of Pabst Blue Ribbon that he lugs
to his trailer for another weekend party of one.

# Barn Razing

I barely notice the changes as,
morning and evening, I drive
past its crumpling bulk:
another shattered windowpane,
six more missing boards,
rows of flapping shingles,
peeling unhinged doors.
Over a century it stood solid,
a ruddy, fodder-crammed ark
housing livestock and tractors.
One rainy day I pull over to see
its great beams hewn in half by
weight and rot and emptiness.
Only a soggy box remains,
stomped sadly to the ground.

# Dust & Ashes

The five-by-five-inch corrugated cube
is labeled TOM in black Sharpie,
a name without a face I'd recognize.

I exhume it from the dresser drawer where
it lies beneath a poppy-covered journal
of poems in my stepmother's cursive.

*He wanted her body, not her soul;*
*She thought he wanted her whole.*
I scan her metered disillusion,

then slit the paper tape, fold back flaps,
find a plastic pouch of grave-gray
dust, her first husband's heirless ashes.

I close the cardboard casket,
bury it deep in a bulging bag
of old tax returns, bank statements,

expired warranties, telephone bills,
chaff the garbage truck will pick up
and drive away next Wednesday.

# Ampersand

Nine months pregnant with possibility,
you arch your conjunctive back, serifs
supporting weary obliques to bear
weight of more, plus, in addition, &tc.

Once part of every student's recitation,
*double-you, ex, why, zee, & per se and,*
you're long since the odd letter out, reduced
to occasional symbol, less than punctuation.

You sit in elliptical contemplation,
rounded bottom seated on baseline,
arms hugging shins to chest, forehead
leaned prayerfully on bony kneecaps

as you ponder tomorrow
& tomorrow &
tomorrow.

# A Grief Preserved

Mourning was past its expiration date,
so we pulled Mason jars from where
they'd collected for years at the back
of kitchen cupboards. As we unscrewed
metal rings and pried off dusty lids,
my sorrow unsealed.

The garbage disposal ran for an hour
while we poured Mom's love down
the drain, my tears mingling with
brine of bread and butter chips,
wax beans, stewed tomatoes,
sweet relish, separated catsup,
cherries faded sickly mauve,
cloudy graying grape juice.

My brother and I rescued the only
wide-mouth quart of pickled peaches,
dark brown, bloated with syrup and spice.
We ate them against Dad's advice,
slurping mushy flesh from stones.
If only cloves could numb our hearts
the way they numbed our tongues.

# Standing in Poet's Corner on Resurrection Day

From where I stand
on these well-trod tiles,
I watch Handel rise first.
He's called from silent
sepulchre by a trumpet
pulsing clarion triads
he composed in life.

Browning stretches,
flexes stiff fingers,
takes up a pen to dash
lines to his Portuguese,
herself newly untombed
in faraway Florence.

Chaucer drapes an arm
across Dickens' shoulders,
and with faces upturned
to the abbey's vaulted sky,
they laugh a light fantastic
to be among so great
a cloud of witnesses.

When Spenser springs
from his secret vault,
a quill tucked behind
one ear and fisting
his fellow poets'
manuscript memorials,
he shreds the priceless
paper into joyous confetti
that scatters like apple blossoms.

Tattered laments land
on Kipling's shoulders,
but Tennyson brushes
them into a cupped palm,
flings them in the face
of Ben Jonson, who
assembles a sonnet
of mourning into dance.

# Sunday Dinner

During today's sermon
my thoughts assemble
around our parents' old table

where we gathered each week
after catechism for a liturgy
of roast beef, buttery potatoes,

gravy, carrots, green beans,
clover rolls, and cherry pie,
condiments of community.

My heart is hungry for a home
that is no more, that is not yet,
until some future Sunday when

we'll gather around Abba's
table, dine on bread and wine,
comfort foods of grace, as if

harsh words were never spoken,
bitter tears were never cried,
no time at all passed since parting.

# The Work of Our Hands

*"Establish the work of our hands for us—*
*yes, establish the work of our hands." (PSALM 90:17)*

We create alone, together,
you below stairs, I above.
Your saw and plane and lathe
hum steady tempos
to my scratching pen
and clicking keyboard.

Your hands grip tools that
block, gouge, hone,
smooth rough wood into
bowls, platters, cups, pens;
shavings of maple, walnut, cherry,
oak curl to the floor until
desired dimensions remain.

My hand grips pen to
block, gouge, hone,
smooth rough words into
sentences, paragraphs, images, moods;
shavings of adverbs, articles, nouns,
verbs curl to the page until
imagined ideas remain.

Geometries echo in my ink,
metaphors echo in your wood;
we work over-under in wonder,
each of us imaging the image
of One who crafted our callings.
Let His pleasure be upon us.

# ACKNOWLEDGMENTS

J ESUS, LIVING WORD, WHEN I WAS TEN YOU CAPTURED MY heart with words, and it has belonged to you ever since. Please accept these poems as a token of my devotion.

Sean, I fell in love with you at a bookstore, and I'm grateful to God for each turn of the page we've shared since then. I look forward to all our adventures yet to come (and I promise I'll do better to obey posted signs and keep back from the edge). Thanks for being my best friend and for always encouraging me to develop the gifts and abilities God has given me.

Ben, being your mom is like looking over God's shoulder as he's crafting the poem of your life. You are such a gift, son, and this world is a more joyful place because you're in it. Keep singing new songs, but remember to play a few old ones for me now and then.

Rich, Julie, Meg, Mark, Tim, and Jane, thanks for being the best older brothers and sisters a kid could hope for. Together we make up a beautiful mosaic of Mom and Dad, and I'm grateful we've had one another to lean on through the long years without them.

Jude, you've been a teacher, mentor, and mama to me. Thanks for your prayers and for always cheering me on as I send my words out into the world.

So many treasured writing friends have surrounded me with encouragement: Sharon, thanks for reading an early draft of this book—it's stronger because you listened. Susie, thanks for embracing me as both a writer and a friend. Julianne, Anuja, and Renee, thanks for your careful critique that helped me shape a number of these poems. Ann, Denise, Tracy, and the entire Breathe community, thanks for celebrating with me.

I also wish to thank the print and online journals in which a number of these poems first appeared:

*Relief Journal*: "A Grief Preserved"
*Presence: A Journal of Catholic Poetry*: "Petoskey Stones"
*Windhover*: "The Language of the Birds"; "Vigil"; "Hidden Manna"
*St. Katherine Review*: "Transfiguration"
*Whale Road Review*: "Back to School"
*Sunlight Press*: "How Much Blue?"; "Larch Song"; "Companion"; "Like Eating a Plum"
*Heart of Flesh*: "It Is Well"
*Local News: Poetry about Small Towns* (anthology): "One Man's Trash"
*Time of Singing*: "Servant"; "Stigmata"; "Brittlebush"; "Climbing Glastonbury Tor"
*Stirring: A Literary Journal*: "My Grandmother's Breakfast"
*Mothers Always Write*: "Melancholidays"; "Home Movies"; "Chapter Break"
*Snapdragon: A Journal of Art & Healing*: "Survivor Guilt"; "Beloved"
*Ancient Paths*: "Pentecost"
*Rocky Mountain Revival* (podcast): "A Daughter's Keepsake"
*The 3288 Review*: "Aslan Makes a Door in the Air"
*Indiana Voice Journal*: "The Work of Our Hands"; "Winter Solstice"; "Prospect Park, Winter 1930"
*Reformed Journal*: "Lines on Holbein's Portrait of Calvin"
*Vine Leaves Literary Journal*: "Mechanics"
*Jesus the Imagination: A Journal of Spiritual Revolution*: "Adam's Rib"
*Poets' Night Out* (Traverse Area District Library): "Ampersand"; "Dad never reads poetry, except"
*Exhale: A Journal of the Breathe Writers Conference*: "Ecclesiology 101"

# ABOUT THE POET

A MY NEMECEK FELL IN LOVE WITH WORDS at an early age. Her work has been nominated for a Pushcart Prize and is featured in numerous print and online journals and anthologies, including *Presence, Relief Journal, Windhover, St. Katherine Review,* and *Whale Road Review.* Amy works as a nonfiction editor for Baker Publishing Group. She lives in West Michigan with her husband, their adult son, and two cats, and when she isn't crafting words, she enjoys traveling to new places with her family and taking long walks in nature.

IRON
PEN

"O that my words were written down!
O that they were inscribed in a book!
O that with an iron pen and with lead
they were engraved on a rock forever!"
—JOB 19:23–24

Outcast and utterly alone, Job pours out his anguish to his Maker. From the depths of his pain, he reveals a trust in God's goodness that is stronger than his despair, giving humanity some of the most beautiful and poetic verses of all time. Paraclete's Iron Pen imprint is inspired by this spirit of unvarnished honesty and tenacious hope.

## OTHER IRON PEN BOOKS

# ABOUT PARACLETE PRESS

PARACLETE PRESS is the publishing arm
of the Cape Cod Benedictine community,
the Community of Jesus. Presenting a full
expression of Christian belief and practice,
we reflect the ecumenical charism of the
Community and its dedication to sacred
music, the fine arts, and the written word.

---

SCAN
TO
READ
MORE

www.paracletepress.com

# YOU MAY ALSO ENJOY THESE ...

www.paracletepress.com